Dinosaurs Alive!

Brachiosaurus

and other dinosaur giants

Jinny Johnson

Illustrated by Graham Rosewarne

W
FRANKLIN WATTS
LONDON•SYDNEY

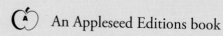 An Appleseed Editions book

First published in 2007 by Franklin Watts

Franklin Watts
338 Euston Road, London NW1 3BH

Franklin Watts Australia
Hachette Children's Books
Level 17/207 Kent St, Sydney, NSW 2000

© 2007 Appleseed Editions

Created by Appleseed Editions Ltd,
Well House, Friars Hill, Guestling,
East Sussex TN35 4ET

Designed by Helen James
Edited by Mary-Jane Wilkins
Artwork by Graham Rosewarne

ISBN 078 07496 7542 4

Dewey Classification: 567.913

A CIP catalogue for this book is available from the British Library.

Photographs by Louie Pslhoyos/CORBIS, James L.Amos/CORBIS

Printed in China

Franklin Watts is a division of Hachette Children's Books

Contents

Dinosaurs' world

A dinosaur was a kind of reptile that lived millions of years ago. Dinosaurs lived long before there were people on Earth.

We know about dinosaurs because many of their bones and teeth have been discovered. Scientists called palaeontologists (pay-lee-on-tol-ojists) learn a lot about the animals by studying these bones.

The first dinosaurs lived about 225 million years ago. They disappeared – became extinct – about 65 million years ago.

Some scientists believe that birds are a type of dinosaur so they say there are still dinosaurs living all around us!

Amargasaurus

4

TRIASSIC
248 to 205 million years ago
Some dinosaurs that lived at this time:
Coelophysis, Eoraptor, Liliensternus,
Plateosaurus, Riojasaurus, Saltopus

EARLY JURASSIC
205 to 180 million years ago
Some dinosaurs that lived at this time:
Crylophosaurus, Dilophosaurus, Lesothosaurus,
Massospondylus, Scelidosaurus, Scutellosaurus

Allosaurus

LATE JURASSIC
180 to 144 million years ago
Some dinosaurs that lived at this time: Allosaurus,
Apatosaurus, Brachiosaurus, Ornitholestes,
Stegosaurus, Yangchuanosaurus

EARLY CRETACEOUS
144 to 98 million years ago
Some dinosaurs that lived at this time: Baryonyx, Giganotosaurus,
Iguanodon, Leaellynasaura, Muttaburrasaurus,
Nodosaurus, Sauropelta

LATE CRETACEOUS
98 to 65 million years ago
Some dinosaurs that lived at this time:
Ankylosaurus, Gallimimus, Maiasaura, Triceratops,
Tyrannosaurus, Velociraptor

Triceratops

Brachiosaurus

Can you believe there was once an animal
that weighed more than 12 elephants?
This was Brachiosaurus, one of the largest,
heaviest creatures that ever lived.

Brachiosaurus was one of a group of giant
plant-eating dinosaurs called sauropods.
These huge, long-necked dinosaurs were
the biggest land animals ever.

This is how you say
Brachiosaurus:
Brak-ee-oh-sore-us

Brachiosaurus's name means 'arm lizard'. Its front legs are much longer than its back legs. This was unusual among sauropods.

BRACHIOSAURUS

Group: sauropods (Sauropoda)

Length: up to 30 metres

Lived in: North America, Africa, Europe

When: Late Jurassic, 155-140 million years ago

Brachiosaurus had a huge body and a long, heavy tail. A fully-grown Brachiosaurus may have weighed an amazing 70 tonnes.

Dinosaurs lived long before there were people on Earth. But here you can see how big a dinosaur was compared with a seven-year-old child.

Inside Brachiosaurus

An animal the size of Brachiosaurus
needed strong bones to carry
its great weight.

Brachiosaurus's neck contained 15 bones, its
ribs were longer than an adult human, and its
leg bones were thick and heavy. Only its head
was small. It measured about 75 centimetres
– about the same as a horse's head.

No one knows why sauropods like
Brachiosaurus were so big, but their
huge size may have helped them
in two ways.

*Brachiosaurus had big fleshy feet with
five toes. There were large claws on the
first toe of each front foot and on the
first three toes of each back foot.*

First, big animals are hard to attack. Few other dinosaurs could win against a full-grown sauropod.

Second, the larger an animal is, the more food it can reach easily.

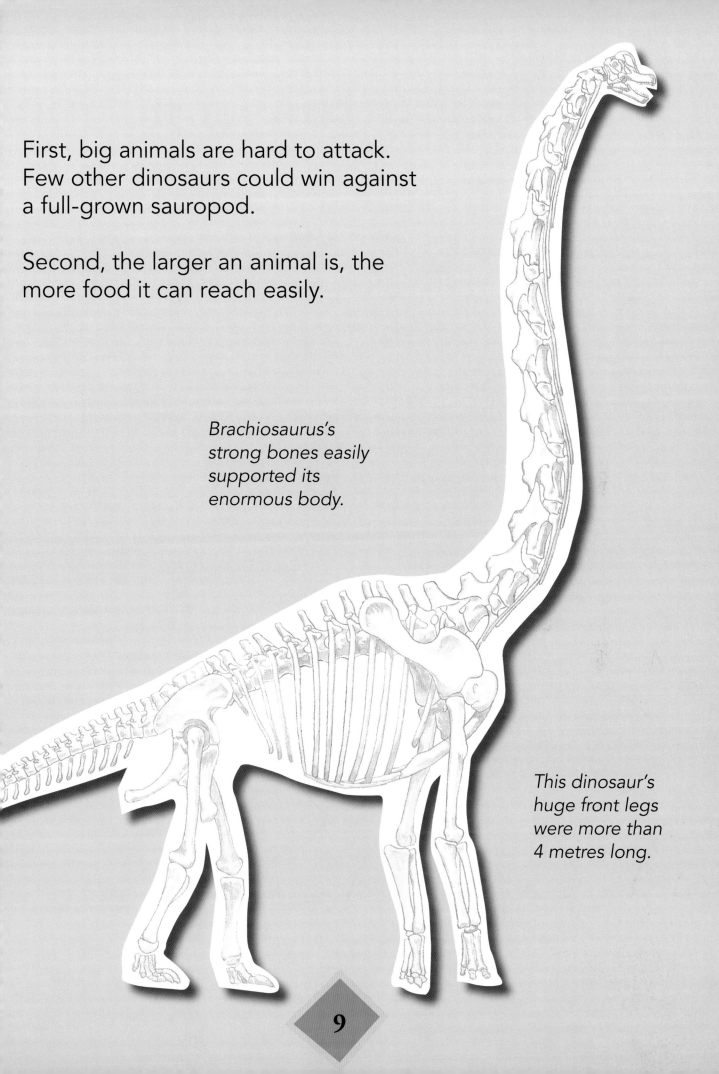

Brachiosaurus's strong bones easily supported its enormous body.

This dinosaur's huge front legs were more than 4 metres long.

Brachiosaurus in action

This enormous animal fed only on plants. Scientists used to think it could reach up into the highest trees, but they now think that sauropods may not have been able to lift their heads very high after all.

Brachiosaurus would still have been able to reach higher than most dinosaurs because of its long front legs. It could take big mouthfuls of fresh green leaves from taller trees than other dinosaurs.

Brachiosaurus may have eaten as much as a tonne of plant food every day. It chopped the leaves from plants with its spoon-shaped teeth.

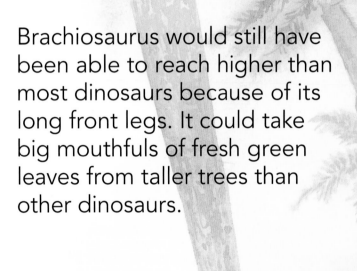

Fossilized dinosaur footprints show that sauropods such as Brachiosaurus moved around in groups called herds. But the dinosaurs were so big and heavy that they couldn't move very fast.

Baby brachiosaurs

Brachiosaurus, like most dinosaurs, laid eggs. The female probably laid as many as 100, each egg the size of a football.

Once a female Brachiosaurus had laid her eggs she left them to hatch by themselves.

A sauropod egg had a hard shell to protect the baby dinosaur growing inside.

The newly-hatched baby sauropods were very small compared with their giant parents and they had to watch out for meat-eating dinosaurs. A baby sauropod made a tasty meal for a hungry predator.

Baby sauropods probably stayed together in groups for safety.

Diplodocus

This mighty dinosaur, with its long neck and long, whip-like tail, was one of the longest land animals that has ever lived.

Diplodocus had bones that were partly hollow, so it was much lighter than Brachiosaurus. Diplodocus weighed only about 11 tonnes.

Diplodocus had a small head and rows of teeth like little pegs. They looked thin and weak, but they were just right for stripping leaves from ferns, its favourite food.

Diplodocus could not chew, but it may have swallowed stones to help grind down the food in its stomach.

DIPLODOCUS

Group: sauropods (Sauropoda)

Length: up to 26 metres

Lived in: North America

When: Late Jurassic, 155-145 million years ago

This is how you say Diplodocus:
Dip-plod-oh-kus

Dinosaur experts think that Diplodocus held its long tail off the ground as it walked.

Camarasaurus

Camarasaurus was a smaller sauropod than Brachiosaurus and Diplodocus, and it had a shorter neck and tail.

Many of Camarasaurus's bones were hollow, so it was lighter than some of its relatives, but it still probably weighed as much as 20 tonnes. Its head was broad and it had large nostrils on the top of its head.

Camarasaurus lived at about the same time as Diplodocus. But its bigger teeth meant it could eat tougher plants than Diplodocus, so the two dinosaurs did not eat the same food.

Camarasaurus lived in herds. The younger dinosaurs stayed close to the adults where they were safe from predators.

CAMARASAURUS

Group: sauropods (Sauropoda)

Length: 23 metres

Lived in: North America

When: Late Jurassic, 150-140 million years ago

This is how you say Camarasaurus:
Kam-ar-a-sore-us

Camarasaurus's large feet had five toes. The inner front toe on each foot had a sharp curved claw.

17

Apatosaurus

Apatosaurus was another huge sauropod.
It was not quite as long as Diplodocus
but much heavier, weighing up to 35 tonnes.

Few creatures would attack a
gigantic animal like this. But
if a hungry tyrannosaur dared
approach, Apatosaurus lashed
out with its long tail. The tail
probably made a cracking sound
like a whip to warn off enemies.

This is how you say
Apatosaurus:
Ah-pat-oh-sore-us

If an attacker did
come near, a blow
from a sauropod's
tail could break its
legs at a stroke.

APATOSAURUS

Group: sauropods (Sauropoda)

Length: up to 21 metres

Lived in: North America

When: Late Jurassic, 154-145 million years ago

A sauropod's long tail was its only weapon against attackers.

19

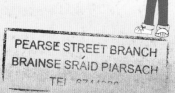

Mamenchisaurus

This sauropod had one of the longest necks of any animal ever. It made up about half the animal's length and had 19 extra-long neck bones.

A giraffe's long neck measures 1.8 metres and contains just seven neck bones.

Dinosaur experts once thought that Mamenchisaurus could stretch up to feed on leaves from the tops of trees, just like giraffes do today. But now they think that the dinosaur could not lift its head very high after all – just enough to reach out for food.

Mamenchisaurus was too big to move around in areas of thick forest. But with its long neck it could reach in and feed on leaves.

MAMENCHISAURUS

Group: sauropods (Sauropoda)

Length: up to 22 metres

Lived in: China

When: Late Jurassic, 155-145 million years ago

This is how you say Mamenchisaurus: Mah-men-kee-sore-us

Seismosaurus

This giant dinosaur was one of the longest land animals ever. It measured 40 metres from its nose to the tip of its long whip-like tail.

The name Seismosaurus means earth-shaking lizard. Like other sauropods, this dinosaur moved in herds, feeding on plants. Its long neck helped it reach food all around so it didn't have to move far.

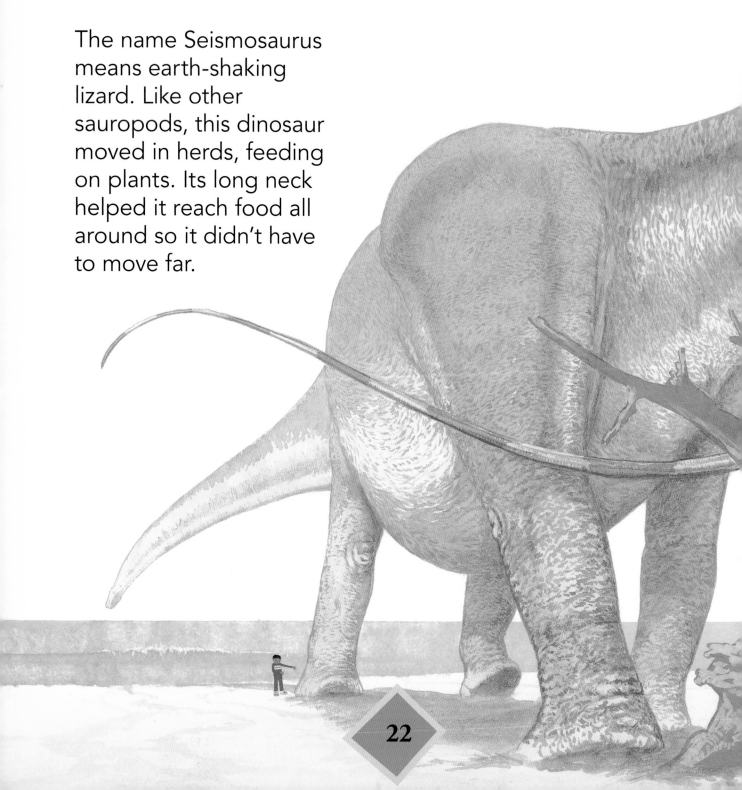

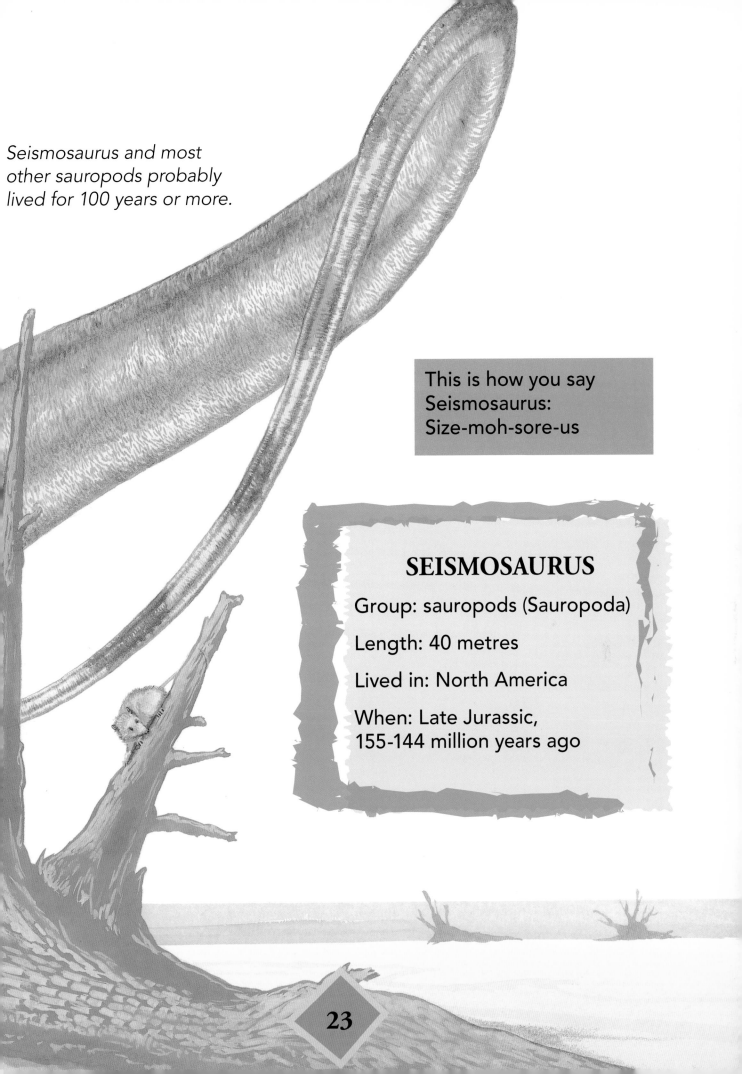

Seismosaurus and most other sauropods probably lived for 100 years or more.

This is how you say Seismosaurus:
Size-moh-sore-us

SEISMOSAURUS

Group: sauropods (Sauropoda)

Length: 40 metres

Lived in: North America

When: Late Jurassic, 155-144 million years ago

Amargasaurus

Amargasaurus was a small sauropod.
It is named after a canyon called La Amarga
in Argentina where its bones were first found.

Amargasaurus had two rows of spines along its backbone, from neck to tail. These may have been covered with skin, making the dinosaur look larger to put off predators. Or the spines may have helped to protect it against attackers.

AMARGASAURUS

Group: sauropods (Sauropoda)

Length: up to 12 metres

Lived in: Argentina

When: Early Cretaceous,
132-127 million years ago

This is how you say
Amargasaurus:
Ah-marg-ah-sore-us

Dinosaur experts think sauropods might have reared up on two legs to reach food or frighten off an enemy.

Alamosaurus

This was one of the last of the sauropods. It lived in North America at a time when most sauropods had already died out.

Alamosaurus belonged to a group of sauropods called titanosaurs. These dinosaurs had shorter tails than Brachiosaurus and tough scales covering their skin. This body armour may have helped to protect them from predators.

ALAMOSAURUS

Group: sauropods (Sauropoda)

Length: up to 21 metres

Lived in: North America

When: Late Cretaceous, 70-65 million years ago

26

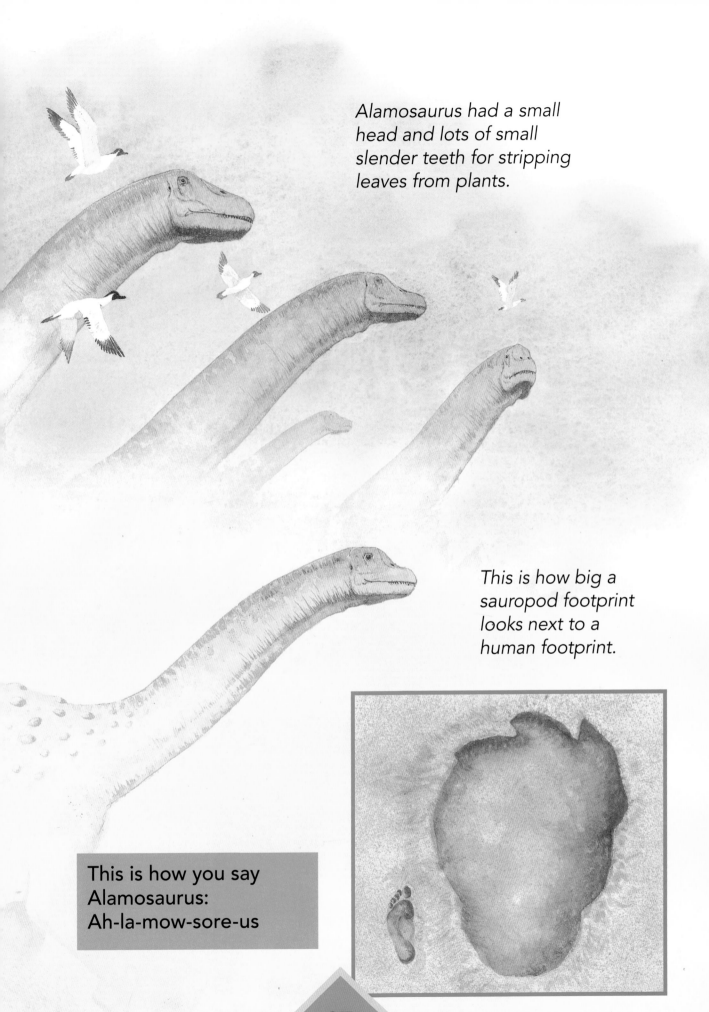

Alamosaurus had a small head and lots of small slender teeth for stripping leaves from plants.

This is how big a sauropod footprint looks next to a human footprint.

This is how you say Alamosaurus:
Ah-la-mow-sore-us

Discovering dinosaurs

Dinosaurs lived long ago – millions of years before the first people. So how do we know so much about them?

One way is by comparing them with similar animals today. Dinosaur experts also learn from fossils such as bones, teeth and eggs. Teeth give clues about what the animals ate. Marks on bones show where muscles were attached and help scientists work out the animal's shape.

This fossilized skull of a horned dinosaur called Protoceratops was found in the Gobi Desert in Mongolia.

A fossil is something that has turned into rock over millions of years. It could be a bone or a tooth. When an animal dies, the soft parts of its body rot away or are eaten by other animals. The hard parts are left. Sometimes these may be buried in mud, in a river or lake bed.

Over millions of years minerals in the water and mud seep into the bones or teeth and replace the original bone. The bones stay the same shape, but gradually become more like rock than bone.

A palaeontologist slowly removes some huge sauropod bones from the rock in Utah, USA.

Words to remember

carnivore
An animal that eats other animals.
Tyrannosaurus was a carnivore.

fossils
Parts of an animal such as bones and teeth that
have been preserved in rock over millions of years.

herbivore
An animal that eats plants. Brachiosaurus was
a herbivore.

herd
A group of animals that usually move and feed together.

palaeontologist
A scientist who looks for and studies fossils to find
out more about the creatures of the past.

predator
An animal that lives by hunting and killing
other animals.

reptile
An animal with a backbone and a dry scaly body.
Most reptiles lay eggs with leathery shells.
Dinosaurs were reptiles. Today's reptiles include
lizards, snakes and crocodiles.

sauropods

A group of long-necked, plant-eating dinosaurs
that includes the largest dinosaurs known.

tyrannosaur

A type of large meat-eating dinosaur such as
Tyrannosaurus which attacked plant-eating dinosaurs.

Index